YOU'RE
THE BEST
INVESTMENT

JENNIFER MULLIGAN

Publish@nowscpress.com
www.PublishWithNOW.com
@nowscpress

Ordering Information:

> Quantity sales. Special discounts are available on quantity purchases by corporations, associations, and others. For details, contact the publisher at the address above.

> Orders by U.S. trade bookstores and wholesalers. Please contact: NOW SC Press: Tel: 813-970-8470 or visit www.PublishWithNOW.com

Printed in the United States of America

First Printing, 2020

ISBN: 978-1-7341809-6-1

DEDICATION

To all the #BossGirls and #EntrepreneurGirls
who are working to reach the next level.

To women and girls who have a dream.
Go after them and take chances.
You can only reach the stars if you push past the clouds.

To my family and my daughter,
you all have been my heart and soul.

CONTENTS

NOTE TO THE READER

As I read my book before it went to press, I heard the echoes of the positive references I gave to my daughter's middle school cheerleading team when I was coaching, encouraging, and teaching them. Those lessons are also a big part of the business fundamentals that I impart in this book. I hope you will enjoy reading about my professional journey and draw your own life lessons from my hard-won lessons. This book is for you—the girls who want to become boss ladies or entrepreneurs. Believe in yourself. You've got this!

#YoureTheBestInvestment

—*Jennifer Mulligan*

1

CHAPTER ONE
BELIEVE YOU CAN DO IT

For a long time, I stared at the long white stick that just changed my entire future. I was seventeen, halfway through my junior year, and pregnant. All of the dreams and choices I'd had just moments before were now infinitely more complicated and, I feared, may even be impossible.

ALL OF THE DREAMS AND CHOICES I'D HAD JUST MOMENTS BEFORE WERE NOW INFINITELY MORE COMPLICATED AND, I FEARED, MAY EVEN BE IMPOSSIBLE.

3

As anyone would in that kind of moment, I panicked at first. I didn't know what I was going to do, never mind how I was going to do it. Raising a child on my own? How was I going to earn a living, go to college, afford an apartment?

I went through the rest of that school year in a kind of numb fog, trying to plan for something completely unexpected. I gave birth to my daughter in August and started my senior year a couple of weeks later. Not in regular high school but in night school, so that I could juggle the baby, work, and homework. While all my friends were worrying about prom dresses and high heels, I was stressing about affording diapers and baby formula.

As my friends moved on the path I thought I would take—prom, graduation, college, dorm life—I felt a fair amount of envy and also like we lived in very different worlds. My friends were supportive but they didn't really understand what I was going through. Every time I envied their freedom and parties, I thought about my daughter and realized, right then and there, that I was doing the most important thing—being a good mom and a good role model.

At seventeen, I was filled with self-doubt. All that normal teenage angst and insecurity was then compounded by being pregnant and thrust into a totally different world than my friends. I didn't know the first thing about babies or raising kids, never mind how to make it all work together. I was terrified that I wasn't going to be able to handle it and debated what road I should take.

But then, one day before my daughter was born, I remember having a conversation with one of my friends. I put my hand on my stomach, atop this new life that depended on me, and told my friend, "I'm going to keep her. I'm going to do this; I *can* do this." In that moment, my mindset shifted and my determination to make it work began to slowly grow.

I'M GOING TO DO THIS; I *CAN* DO THIS.

START WITH YOUR MINDSET

When I was little, I was in Girl Scouts. I started with Daisies, worked my way up to Brownies, and then finally became a Girl Scout. During the annual cookie sale, I remember being a very young girl and having to go up to total strangers and ask them if they wanted to buy some Thin Mints. I could have been paralyzed with fear. Instead, I convinced myself that this was easy—it was just talking, after all, something I did every day—and I could do it.

It helped that I was outgoing. As a young girl, I ran a lemonade stand, organized our neighborhood band, and tried out for the dance team. I guess I had that entrepreneurial, risk-taking spirit early on. I might not know how to do something or be afraid I wouldn't be able to do it, but I discovered that everything I attempted went much better if I pictured myself doing it and told myself I could. Even as a little girl, I was working to create a can-do mindset, unaware of how important that would be years down the road.

That positive, I-can-do-it spirit got put to the test when my daughter was one and I was barely nineteen. I had landed a position as a teller at an in-store bank and part of my job was to go out to the grocery shoppers to convince them to come to the bank and sign up for an account. It was intimidating and a lot of people didn't take this young blonde seriously, but I was determined to provide a good living for my daughter which drove me, every day, to do my best. I knew why I was there and what was on the line, so it spurred me to buckle down and conquer any fears I might have.

What is your reason for being in your job? For doing what you do? When you find your why, that becomes the foundation of your belief in yourself. Having an important, personal reason for what you are doing helps you dig deep for that fuel you need when you face a setback or your goal seems impossibly out of reach.

A ROADMAP TO GET TO YOUR WHY

1. Think of pivotal stories from your past and present that motivate you to do what you do.

2. What do these stories have in common? Do you like to help people? Do you find purpose

in creating art or music? Do you feel strongly about making an impact on your community?

3. Create a WHY statement. Write it down and post it somewhere you can see it every day so, when times get tough, you remember your why and keep going.

If you think about it, having the right mindset applies to more than just a career. If you want to buy your first house, it will take a lot longer if you don't have a money mindset. Meaning, an overriding attitude about money that guides every financial decision you make. Your eyes are focused on that cute four-bedroom Cape Cody style-house on the cul de sac, so you think twice about buying a jet ski or that daily Starbucks habit. When your mindset focuses, you are more confident about your goals and every decision is made that much easier.

WHEN YOU HAVE THE RIGHT MINDSET, IT SHOULD BECOME THE FOUNDATION OF ALL DECISIONS YOU MAKE.

What's the opposite of having a money mindset? Making decisions out of fear and impulsivity, feeling defeated, or procrastinating and not working toward your goals. Pretty much the exact same things we do when we are faced with obstacles we aren't sure we can overcome—right?

That's *why* it's so important to know *why* you are working where you work, *why* you are moving to the state you've chosen, *why* you make any major life change. When you know *why*, you can turn to that touchstone to give you the strength to make your next move.

YOUR *WHY* SHOULD BE YOUR NORTH STAR.
THE COMPASS THAT GUIDES EVERYTHING YOU DO.

CREATE ACTION STEPS

One of the badges I most wanted to earn in Girl Scouts was archery. I had never been around a bow and arrow and my father didn't hunt, so I was a little intimidated by the archery set. I convinced myself I could do it, then learned everything I could about how to shoot an arrow. From there, I created action steps in my head—take my stance, raise the bow, aim well, draw my elbow back, release—so that I was ready when the time came to shoot. It took a lot of practice and deep breaths, but I eventually learned a new skill and earned that badge.

That's basically what I have done all my life—set a goal, decided I could achieve it, and then created the necessary action steps to make it happen. When I was looking at real estate as an investment, I searched the area for properties, secured the financing, and then flipped the property for a profit. Another time, I wanted to build better relationships with the Federal

Reserve and state regulators so that I had those relationships in place as I moved up the ladder. I managed to expand my network and connections by going to one of my peers, who helped me connect at both the state and federal levels.

There will be challenges when you set out to achieve your goals. I give myself time and space to process each step. At work, I don't like to hop from one meeting to another. I need at least thirty minutes of space—essentially, some breathing time— to assess the meeting I just left and plan for the next one. I'll write down any notes, recap the main points, then take a minute to plan my next steps and what tasks will be delegated. That organization helps me feel prepared for the next challenge.

DON'T BE AFRAID TO TAKE A MOMENT TO PAUSE, REGROUP, AND THINK ABOUT YOUR NEXT STEP. SOMETIMES THAT'S NECESSARY TO MAKE SURE YOU CONTINUE MOVING IN THE RIGHT DIRECTION.

Sometimes it can be hard for women to believe in themselves and not listen to their self-doubt and the disbelief from others. We aren't taught to celebrate our strengths. However, if you learn to do that, something wonderful will happen along your path to success. The stereotypical advice says to reward yourself with a spa day and, while that's great, truly celebrating your strengths means changing the way you talk to yourself.

Women tend to see their strengths as weaknesses—like seeing determination and perceiving it as pushiness. Use a mental thesaurus and change the words in your head to more positive and empowering options. For instance, when someone calls you stubborn, see that as a positive trait of determination, which is a building block for achieving your next goal.

Also look at how others treat you. Their respect and esteem for you are a good marker for where your strengths lie. Do they often tell you that you are a good leader? Great at communicating? Organized? Use that to create a vision for the path ahead, whether it be one that leads to becoming a business owner or politician, or something altogether different. That's using your connectivity, making it work for you and *through* you.

MEET CHALLENGES HEAD-ON

When I was twenty-three, I went on a job interview where the interviewer questioned my banking knowledge. "Do you know what stock options are? Pro forma?" he asked. Maybe it was all those late nights, missed parties, and structured days, but I was confident when I answered him. I was ready for, and knew I could meet, the challenge of his questions. When I got into this industry, I made it a point to be familiar with everything surrounding leadership: Company culture, diversity, growth, benefits, stock options, flexibility, technology—basically all the things that were important in making up the fabric of every company. It was part of my commitment to a bigger picture, something bigger than me. I knew that investing in my education in this industry would be a strength that would serve me for a long time to come.

I had goals, a plan, and a list of accomplishments I wanted to achieve, so I missed those parties and late nights. Instead, I dedicated my time to investing in myself and my education.

EXECUTE AND MOVE FORWARD

There have been several times when my entire life has been uprooted, either from becoming a single mom or moving to a brand-new state. I was in unfamiliar, scary territory and I fell back on those skills I learned as a young girl every time—get my mindset right, create a plan, then execute it and move forward.

I could have easily given up at any point, especially in those difficult early years. Thankfully, my parents were a big help but, in the end, the responsibility was all on my shoulders. I juggled a job with nighttime diaper changes and running to daycare. I remember several years where I barely slept, trying to keep up with it all.

To be honest, it took a constant focus to maintain my can-do mindset. I was embarrassed to be such a young, unmarried mother. Society often judges single moms and many people judged me. I didn't want them to think I was some kind of failure; I wanted them to see the confident, capable woman I was becoming. As I cultivated that belief inside myself, I learned to withhold personal information to construct the image

I wanted others to see. I created, essentially, a platform for marketing Jennifer Mulligan. If I saw a woman with a baby in her grocery cart, I told her I had a baby at home without going into the details of how or why. It established a commonality with potential customers and a way for me to build a stronger outside while I was working on the inside.

I also made sure I was held accountable, not just to others but to myself. When things got tough, I reminded myself of the bigger goal. Goals are achieved, not just through mindset and persistence but through accountability. That allows you to measure and mark the milestones you achieve.

Everything I had done up to that point in my life, however, prepared me for those difficult early years with my little girl. When I was on the dance team in high school, I learned to keep performing with a smile on my face no matter if I was exhausted or worried about grades. I leaned on my teammates when I needed them and used the rigors of practice to keep me going when things got tough. If that happens to you, then try these steps to get back on track:

1. Take a deep breath, process, and regroup.

2. Revisit your WHY. Say it out loud.

3. Break down the next steps into small, achievable goals.

4. Tackle your action plan one step at a time.

Regardless of where you are in your life right now, start believing you can achieve whatever your dream may be—you'll be closer than you were the day before. Your mindset will have you making the right deposits—practice, routine, discipline—for whatever is necessary so you go from where you are today to where you want to be. That's what this book is here to help you do; find that inner reserve that helps you climb mountains no one ever thought you could tackle.

A SELF INVESTMENT DEPOSIT SLIP

Close your eyes and picture yourself accomplishing your goal. Imagine every aspect of it, from where you are to what you are hearing and seeing. Make this a vivid visualization. Then ask yourself—what steps do I need to take to get there? When you are done, open your eyes, create an action plan, and execute it!

CHAPTER TWO
THE IMPORTANCE OF DISCIPLINE AND ROUTINE

If you ever want a challenge in teaching the importance of discipline and routine, volunteer to lead a cheerleading team made up of teenagers. The girls I coached were thirteen to fifteen, and they were more focused on their phones or whether that boy in Algebra was interested than learning the routines we were practicing. I spent a lot of time talking to them about the potential fallout from failing to practice—we could lose a competition, the team could break up, and worst of all, someone could get hurt.

I learned early on that different girls required different motivators, whether it was leaving practice early after mastering a skill or getting a candy bar for trying a particularly difficult move. I also leaned on the girls who were natural leaders because they would inspire their teammates to try harder. I sometimes had the equivalent of a pop quiz and would randomly call on one of the girls and ask her to lead the team in a particular move. Knowing they could be called to the mat at any time quickly taught all the girls to mind their Ps and Qs.

It was an easy connection for them to make because they understood that not warming up or stretching would lead them to pulling a muscle. Not practicing could lead to a teammate being hurt. The girls with experience helped the ones who weren't as practiced, which was a direct result of the team building we did. If something happened within the team, I held them all accountable as a team. That created a group with a vested interest in success, and gave other girls the courage to step up and point out things we needed to work on. Every single practice, we worked at being disciplined and ready, with the girls learning how to lean on each other and communicate well.

START WITH A ROUTINE

These were skills I had had to master when I was just a little older than the girls on the squad. I had a new baby, school, and a job. I had to create a schedule and a routine, and then stick to it, or everything else fell apart. I woke up every morning at four and got ready for the day before my daughter woke up. I picked out clothes and made my lunch the night before as I often worked long into the night on schoolwork while my daughter was asleep. I leaned on all the resources I had, whether it was daycare, my family, or my friends. They were my cheer team when I hit a rough patch or needed a break for a few hours.

Although I was always fairly disciplined when I was young, having a baby who wasn't necessarily on a predictable schedule changed so many things in my life. I created a routine from the minute she was born so that I could more or less predict when she needed to sleep or eat, and so that she could also depend on the structure of her days. Numerous studies show the importance of a predictable routine for babies because it teaches them that they can depend on their needs being met.

The routine gave me the structure to build my new life. As I worked my way up in the in-store bank from teller to assistant manager, I leaned on the Florida Bankers training program to enhance my skillset. I took courses in retail banking, cash flow, business principles, etc., giving me the required education to move into a bigger sales and operations role with another company.

PRACTICE IS ESSENTIAL

My new job was focused on planting new banks up and down Florida's west coast. The bank had targeted certain markets and demographics which required data gathering and analysis. My daughter was in preschool and I was juggling motherhood with traveling, which meant I had to be even more prepared for meetings because my time was that much more limited.

It was an intimidating time for me. I was a young, single mom who was staying in hotels, talking to strangers, and building business relationships. I was also blonde and female and faced some definite age and sex discrimination. In order to beat those stereotypes and be successful, I knew I had to be ready.

I overprepared for meetings because I knew many of the people in those boardrooms only saw my age and hair color. I practiced in the mirror until I knew how I planned to enter the room, what I would say while I was there, and how to close the meeting. I found serious power in visualization because it gave me a mental picture of the entire process. When I coached my sales teams or worked with the cheerleading squad, I did the same thing: *Let's talk through the schedule. What prompts do we need to look for and how will the finished product look?*

I taught the girls how to build their own confidence levels. It empowered them, which is a skill they will use all their lives. Girls today often struggle with gaining confidence, asking for help, or being strong enough to push back when something isn't right or they are being disrespected.

CONFIDENCE EMPOWERS GIRLS,
A SKILL THEY WILL USE ALL THEIR LIVES.

I'm glad to see that the universe is changing and women are breaking the glass ceiling more often. For me, getting to the top was about building a network of people who were smarter than me, knowing when to ask for help, and not being afraid to take risks. Practice gave me confidence, discipline and routine gave me the sweat equity I needed, and courage pushed me to the next step.

KNOW YOUR PRIORITIES

We all face choices, every single day, in terms of where we are going to focus our efforts. I remember a compliance exam I had to take early in my career. Instead of studying for it, I procrastinated and crammed for the test the night before. I wasn't ready and failed the exam. I learned a valuable lesson—I had allowed distractions to get in the way of my goals.

1. Set Your Goals: It's difficult, if not impossible, to develop a routine, then practice and develop discipline, if you don't know where you want to go. Don't be afraid to set big goals because you can achieve far more than you think. Make a list of the smaller goals that will get you to that

pinnacle and the skills you need to get from point A to point B.

2. **Make Room for What's Important:** My daughter was my top priority, with my career coming in second. I made my decisions based on what was most important to me. That priority became a barometer for every choice I made.

3. **Block out Distractions:** There is so much noise in our world today, between social media, advertising, and other people. It's easy to get distracted by what's happening on Facebook or the newest Netflix series. Go back to number one and two—what is your goal and what is most important to you? Do those distractions fit into either of those categories? If not, don't give away your precious time.

4. **Be Comfortable with Saying No:** As women, we have a tendency to not want to rock the boat or upset other people. I've learned to steer my ship based on my priorities. For instance, someone I know well recently invited me to a networking event. As much as I was thankful and appreciative for the invitation, I knew I didn't have time. When this happens, I simply say *I'm unavailable* or *I'm committed elsewhere.* I don't need to explain or justify my choices to other people, and neither do you. It's completely okay to say, *I'm unavailable that day* and leave it at that.

REMEMBER: 'NO' IS A COMPLETE SENTENCE.

Every single one of us already has these skills inside us. We can be disciplined, practiced, courageous, and strong—but only if we start by believing we can be. None of the advice in this book will help you if you don't start with the belief that you are capable and that your goals are important.

A woman who used to work for me asked me to dinner last week. She thanked me for giving her a chance all those years ago and for helping her advance in her career. She was now a mom and asked my advice on how working parents juggle everything. I told her to start by ignoring her critics because people are going to question your skills and decisions, no matter what.

BELIEVE IN YOURSELF, FIRST AND FOREMOST.

DON'T FORGET TO HAVE FUN, TOO

I'm in the banking industry and in the business sector, both of which are usually thought of as the exact opposite of fun. I don't party with my customers, but I do make sure to embrace the relationships and to keep things interesting.

For example, I once had a customer who owned a farm. They provided produce for restaurants throughout the country. I went out to the farm, met the family, tried some of their food, and then brought the food back to my office. It was a way to promote business in that community while also supporting them and supporting my team.

For me, keeping things fun and interesting is part of relationship building. People bank with people they know and trust. When I met the family that owned the farm, they got to know me, and I got to know them. That built the foundation of a relationship where they could trust that I always had their best interests at heart. That's a critical component of everything you do in life—because if you don't build those relationships, you won't have the support structure you need later. Discipline is wonderful, but so is opening up enough to let people get to know you.

Ever since I was seventeen, I have dealt with doubters and haters who asked me "How are you going to do it? How are you going to be a good wife, a good mother, a good employee?" I told them to simply watch me. I learned to be okay with being imperfect and with standing up for myself. I kept coming back to rules number one and two—goals and priorities. I put my energy into my priorities and ignored the distractions that tried to derail me from my path. Most importantly, I believed in myself.

It's the same with those thirteen-year-old girls who are so wrapped up in the immediate drama of what's on their phones and Facebook feeds that they can't see what's coming down the road. It took a lot of time and energy to help them create that vision of what they wanted for their futures. When things got off course or something threatened to upset them, I would tell them to slow down and recast that vision.

SOMETIMES, JUST TAKING A SECOND TO BREATHE AND REFOCUS IS ALL YOU NEED TO GET BACK ON YOUR FEET.

A SELF INVESTMENT DEPOSIT SLIP

Remember: 'No' is a complete sentence. Set your boundaries and stick to them because your wants, needs, and goals are important too!

CHAPTER THREE
RELATIONSHIP BUILDING

For as long as I can remember, I watched my mother build her business. She invested in it—and herself—over and over again, building it a little at a time. My mother was outgoing and smart, and she worked with other people in the small business community to bring them together, so that they all helped each other. She built relationships and those relationships endured all the years she was in business.

She worked the late nights, spent the weekends doing her profit and loss statements, and in short poured everything she had into that business. From her, I learned a work ethic and the power of working for and on yourself. I also learned the importance of working with other people, and how connecting with the right people can make all the difference.

KNOW THE POWER OF PARTNERSHIP

My mother had a business partner, and in the 80s, that women-owned business dynamic was much more unique than it is today. My mother brought me in part-time to lick the envelopes (which tasted disgusting, by the way), for the mailers that she sent out to other business owners. She believed in collaborating with other entrepreneurs, to better everyone's bottom line.

I watched my mother make her marriage and her business partnership work. There were disagreements and financial struggles, but there were also times to celebrate. At a fairly young age, I learned that nothing is ever perfect in business or in a relationship, but you can keep the engine moving if you have teamwork.

That's the secret to making any kind of working relationship a strength to the business—teamwork. I had to learn how to be part of a team and, as I climbed the corporate ladder, I had to build my own teams. There are a few keys to making a team work:

- Communication: The number-one component of a strong team and partnership is communication. People don't always listen or they might misinterpret something, so maintaining a strong level of communication can make a huge difference. If anything, I tend to over communicate because I want to be sure people get the information they need. With the cheer team, my assistant coach and I both made sure to repeat information. Parents with three kids are busy and could easily miss something. By over communicating, everyone on the team is on the same page. We covered every element of a competition, from who was holding which position to who was going to be helping with makeup. That ensured no detail was missed. In my industry, covering all the details is vitally important and accurate, timely, and thorough communication is crucial.

- Activities: Building a team doesn't just happen. It requires leadership that brings the team together. With the cheer girls, I started by making sure every girl had everyone else's phone number. We got together once a week as a team at a local restaurant, just to have fun, give out a few awards for spirit or execution, and build our camaraderie. I do the same with my teams at the bank because it helps everyone's working relationships when we focus on teamwork. We do some kind of an icebreaker every year, whether it's a scavenger hunt or a *Survivor*-themed adventure. Just because we're bankers doesn't mean we can't have fun.

- Rank Priorities: When I work with a team, one of the first things I set in place is the team's priorities. A partnership doesn't work if the two partners have different priorities. A cheer pyramid will fall if some of the squad is focusing on other things. When I worked with the cheer team, we talked a lot about the priority of the squad. Was the priority winning or was it making sure no one got hurt? Which was more important? That helped them focus on routine, practice, and safety, instead of some trophy.

- Evaluate: Check in with your team members. Create feedback loops to learn how the team can function better as a whole. Listen to each other. Start practicing the idea: Leaders speak last. In your evaluation, make sure team members feel heard.

If you notice, the elements I've outlined to make a team work spell out the word CARE. Above all else, team members should not only care about Communication, Activities, Ranking Priorities and Evaluating the team, they should also learn to *care* for each other. This requires creating a safe space for your team, whether that's in your business or on your cheer squad.

A few months ago, I was in a foursome golf scramble. At first, we were all talking and laughing and then I realized that we really could do well if we worked together. I asked the other women about our strategy and we collaborated on a way to play to our strengths. We communicated and worked together—and won.

CARE ABOUT EACH OTHER.

If you communicate and work hard, people are going to understand that you are doing the best you can. That will encourage everyone to put forth their best effort and, in the end, create more success for the group as a whole.

FIND GOOD MENTORS

I was young and didn't know anything about banking when I interviewed with that first in-store branch in Brandon. Anita, the branch manager there, saw something in me and gave me a chance. She encouraged me, guided me, and helped me build my confidence. A mentor like that is invaluable because they can guide you in the right direction and help pave the way when you aren't sure what to do next.

A GOOD MENTOR WILL GUIDE YOU AND HELP BUILD YOUR CONFIDENCE.

Anita is not the only mentor who helped me out along the way. When my daughter was young, I took a leap of faith and moved to Chicago, even though I didn't have a job. I had an interview at JP Morgan Chase. Colleen, the woman interviewing me, sat back in her chair and said, "Jennifer, your resume is impressive but you are well overqualified for what we have here."

I nodded. "You're right, but I'm willing to take a few steps back in order to jump forward." This was when the market was crashing and I knew I just needed to get my foot in the door. She saw that hard-working, can-do spirit in me, took a chance, and hired me.

At the time, Chase was in the process of buying Washington Mutual. Colleen offered me a position as a training manager, a job where I was tasked with going into a Washington Mutual and help them convert to the Chase corporate culture. The two cultures were very different and I had to learn a lot about Chicago and Chase to succeed in that position. After I finished at that location, I was moved to another branch in a crime-ridden area. I even learned Mandarin in order to converse with the staff and customers. It was a challenge, but I put everything I had into it because my priorities were long-term success and a solid financial future for myself and my daughter.

Colleen was impressed and promoted me to handling conversion at the John Hancock center, a huge leap up the Chase ladder. Moving to that branch helped me learn to step up more for myself and to realize that I wasn't going to go as far as I wanted to with Chase. When I was offered another merger/acquisition position in West Michigan, I took it.

YOU'VE GOT TO STEP UP FOR YOURSELF AND YOUR PRIORITIES.

Colleen liked to use football analogies when she talked to people, which only helped build the team atmosphere. She gave me a chance to prove myself, and I was determined to do just that. Sometimes a door is opened for you. It might not be the perfect situation right off the bat, but you can grow and flourish over time with the right leadership and opportunities. Anita and Colleen were the mentors who helped provide that leadership for me.

BE A PROBLEM SOLVER

One of my favorite parts about working in banking is sitting back and listening to business owners and customers. I realized how many Americans live paycheck to paycheck and how easily a business can drop into the red. In today's climate and after the national months-long shutdown, it's even easier. Small businesses are especially vulnerable and need someone who is in their corner.

I watched my mother with her company, Welcome Newcomer, help other companies increase their revenue. She helped them with their advertising and marketing, which in turn brought them more customers and more business. It's no wonder she and her business partner were named Brandon Business Owner of the Year in 2000. When I got into the banking industry, I knew I wanted to be able to do the same.

Banking, however, is a business that is built on trust and relationships. People want to know and be confident that the person who is handling their money has their best interests in mind. The very first time I approached a busy mom in the grocery store to ask if she wanted to open a checking account at our tiny in-store branch, I realized that I needed to start by building a relationship. We would chat and I got to know the customers, while they got to know me. When they opened an account, they knew there would be a friendly face helping them with their deposits.

Part of building relationships is about knowing your strengths and weaknesses, and then building on the things that you are good at. A lot of those answers come through self-discovery. When I work with my teams, I give them tasks that help them see that maybe they're good at time management, or organization, or creativity.

IT'S ALL ABOUT SEEING WHAT PEOPLE ARE GOOD AT AND THEN GIVING THEM THE OPPORTUNITY TO SHINE IN THAT CAPACITY.

I've always been good at talking to people and at getting people to talk to me. That led to my first job and helped me advance in the banking industry. Later, that gave me the ability to identify talent and then build people up, helping them to believe in themselves.

In the last week, I've gone back to my relationships. I dusted off the Rolodex and reached out to the relationships I established long ago. For some people, it had been many, many years since we last talked. I fast-tracked and had moved up so quickly I forgot to reach out and talk to people to see how they were doing. The downtime during the pandemic gave me a moment to reach out to people who used to work for me and ask them how their families were doing, how they were, and where they were in their careers. Reestablishing those connections helped plug me back in with people I respected and cared about.

One of my weaknesses is not being conscientious about maintaining those relationships. However, as the years have gone by and I've gone through a number of transitions, I have become more focused on rekindling those connections and helping support people wherever I can.

I've also been on the receiving end as former employees of mine have reached out to ask how I'm doing and what's next for me. It was awesome to hear from them, to feel their support, and hear their advice. No matter who you are or where you are on the corporate ladder, don't forget the people who helped you get there.

A SELF INVESTMENT DEPOSIT SLIP

This week, reach out to three people from your past and reestablish that connection. Ask how they are doing and how you can help them. Maintaining those connections can be the link you need when you need to make a career pivot.

CHAPTER FOUR
CROSS-TRAIN YOURSELF

One of the most harrowing moments on the Netflix docuseries *Cheer* is when one of the flyers takes a tumble and breaks her arm right before the biggest competition of the team's year. It could have been a disaster and could have eliminated the team before they even arrived, but the coach had prepared for just such an eventuality by having the team members cross train. Another team member took her place and the team's performance didn't suffer (I won't give away the ending, though).

Cross-training isn't just about knowing other positions within the company—cross-training gives you options and choices. It's one of the best things you can do for yourself because it keeps you from ever being stuck anywhere. I have worked in several industries and positions, which has given me a wide network of connections and choices whenever I have had to make a career move.

CROSS-TRAINING GIVES YOU OPTIONS AND CHOICES.

Women struggle with believing they can leave a situation, whether it's a bad relationship, a bad apartment, or a bad job. They feel stuck and they tolerate a situation much longer than they should. If you are cross-trained in other jobs and other industries, *you are never stuck.*

You can leave a hostile work environment. You can take a risk on a dream. You can try a new career. In addition, cross-training:

1. Makes you more valuable in the workforce

2. Gives you a continuous safety net

3. Helps you understand other points of view

4. Opens more doors and opportunities

5. Empowers you to walk away and start new

CONFIDENCE MAKES ALL THE DIFFERENCE

You can have all the cross-training in the world, but it won't work without confidence. That's the fuel that powers you forward when you are embarking on something new or unfamiliar. Believe you can do it and trust that you have already put those pennies in the bank with your partnerships, routine, and discipline. The training is there—trust it. I told the girls on competition days the same thing—trust all the work you have already put in.

CONFIDENCE IS A SKILL. YOU CAN LEARN TO BE CONFIDENT. YOU CAN PRACTICE CONFIDENCE DAILY.

In the last few months, I've been moving in new directions in my career. To do that, I reached out to many people I knew in the past for counsel and advice. Their words helped wake up my confidence and get it roaring again. These people are telling me I can do it, that I will be successful. *Jennifer, think higher of yourself. We all know who you are and you should, too.* It doesn't matter how far we go in our careers or personal lives, everyone will suffer days of doubt. When that happens, go back to the people who knew you when. They will be that cheering section that says "Let's go. Let's do this." Find a few good people who will introduce you to a few good people and you'll have that valuable network in place.

DON'T BE AFRAID TO ASK FOR HELP.
WE ALL NEED CHEERLEADERS IN OUR LIVES.

WHAT ARE YOUR KEY SKILLS?

Early in my career, I met someone who had worked at Chuck E. Cheese. He was people-friendly, smart, outgoing—and perfect for working in the bank. You might think that sounds crazy but I didn't hire him for his ability to handle toddlers having a meltdown. I hired him because he had the skill set I was looking for.

Banking is a relationship business. As I've said before, people bank with people they trust. I am always looking for individuals who have those people skills and who can deliver on the relationship piece. That's a huge part in the overall success of the bank, so it's the first key skill I look for when I'm hiring.

It's important to do that self-evaluation about your skill set. Maybe you're an introvert or someone who likes to work with data or technology. Cross-train in areas that feed into that skill set. When you need to make a career shift, you will be working within your comfort zone whether you are working at an insurance agency or a manufacturing company.

CHOOSE JOBS THAT FIT WHO YOU ARE AS A PERSON.

If you're struggling with this, take an inventory of your life. Ask yourself:

- What went well and what held you back from taking the next step?

- What positive things did you accomplish?

- What boards or committees did you serve on?

- What values do you bring to your organization?

- Are there some volunteer or board opportunities that can help bring you to the next level?

If you're already doing that volunteer work, are they making use of your best key skills in the organization? One of the groups I volunteered with put me in charge of planning birthday parties. That's definitely not my strength, so I had a conversation with the group about a role that would better utilize my skillset.

If you don't have the key skills you need to accomplish your goals, look for someone who does. Play to your strengths and let others help in areas you know you are weak. Also, never be afraid to ask for help. My older sister wanted to buy a house and called me because I understand the banking and real estate side of the transaction. We looked at the house she wanted and, when it came time to negotiate, I told her she could ask for a reduction in the realtor's commission because she wasn't using her own realtor. My sister needed a little wiggle room to cover the closing costs but she was nervous about the negotiations, so I handled it. The realtor agreed to the commission reduction and my sister was overjoyed.

IF YOU DON'T ASK, THE ANSWER WILL ALWAYS BE NO.

BUT I'M BAD AT MATH

There have been many times when people on my team or people I just hired came to me and said, "I can't do this job."

My response?

"I can teach you."

When you find the right mentors and guides, they will teach you instead of leaving you to flounder on your own. They will lead you in a way that allows for self-discovery and for you to believe in yourself.

There is always someone out there who has the strengths you need to cultivate. Go through your contact list and call on those people. Be confident enough to pick up the phone and ask for their advice or help. Learn to lean on the team you already have in your life.

Women tend to avoid negotiating over money because they don't feel comfortable saying, "That's not going to work for me." With my sister's real estate transaction, I encouraged her to stay strong and not put all of her financial cards on the table. By standing firm on the dollars and cents, it helped build her confidence in that moment.

Many women today have been brought up in a society that taught them to be deferential, to not stand up and take charge. We have to break that cycle and do a better job of setting our boundaries and expectations. Too often we default to saying, '*I can't do it*', or '*I'm stuck*', or '*This is too much*' because we aren't confident in our leadership ability (it all goes back to confidence). More times than I can count, I had a girl on the team who would say she couldn't do this or that. In reality, she was fully capable of executing that turn or flip—but she was scared to try something new.

SEE YOUR OWN VALUE

When you cross-train, you make yourself more valuable—not just to employers, but to yourself. You learn new skills which, in turn, feed your can-do spirit and you begin to believe you can take on a big challenge.

Think about a marathon runner. No runner started off running 26.2 miles on her first outing. Every single runner started running a few feet, then a few miles, then did different runs to build different strengths. She trained on hills and trails, experiencing different terrains and weather conditions, so that she was ready for whatever comes her way on race day.

That's the key to cross-training. It prepares you mentally. A change in direction or a change in the weather won't stop you because you'll already know you are capable of tackling it. I work in a male-dominated industry and have learned that it's okay to keep my cards close to the vest and not be that deferential pleaser. It has taken years of practicing to master different situations and believing in both myself and my knowledge base to be able to hold my own, regardless of what comes my way.

CROSS-TRAINING PREPARES YOU MENTALLY.

The more you see your own value, the more other opportunities will come to you. You have to be okay to sing your own praises and to talk to people in your network. If you are struggling to do that, pull out your resume. Look at all you have accomplished! Look at how you have hopped into different lanes and not just landed there, you succeeded. You have been successful and you have what it takes to do that again.

For moms who are just getting back into the workforce, that personal resume check is even more vital. They've spent a lot of time caring for their kids and often struggle to see how that translates into the workforce. Those skills of organization, scheduling, and multitasking are all fantastic for the workforce. I once hired a guy who ran a seed company. When he asked me why I was bringing him into banking, I explained that he knew how businesses worked and he would be fantastic on our corporate side. He could learn the banking end of it—but he had the inherent knowledge from his life experience that was vital in his position.

Years ago, a woman in the organization business helped me with my closets. Now, she's doing business consulting because she has worked with numerous businesspeople over the years and used that time as an opportunity to cross-train herself. She's reaching out to her business contacts to help expand her network and leverage those connections. When she calls, I think about two things: How can she bring value to me? And how can I bring value to her?

BUSINESS RELATIONSHIPS ARE ABOUT GIVING AND RECEIVING. WHAT VALUE ARE YOU GIVING? WHAT VALUE ARE YOU RECEIVING?

It's not just about helping ourselves, it's also about helping others and appreciating their skills and work ethic. On the cheer team, I made sure everyone knew all the positions so that they could appreciate how hard the bases worked or the skill the flyers had. That helped the entire team anticipate the needs of their teammates and to think strategically. Cross-training is the definition of teamwork because you all know and appreciate each other—and then can plan ahead for what one department might need or encounter.

IT'S NOT ALWAYS ABOUT HELPING OURSELVES.
IT'S ALSO ABOUT HELPING OTHERS.

WHAT IF IT DOESN'T WORK OUT?

What if you do all the right things, get all the right training, make the right connections and your new venture still doesn't work out?

Congratulate yourself anyway. You got up, got dressed, went out, and did it. That alone is a huge part of restoring your confidence so that you are ready to move down the next path.

When my sister was trying to decide to buy a house or renew her lease, we sat down on the beach and made a pros and cons list. She asked me, '*What if it doesn't work out?*' I asked her, '*But what if it does?*'

WHAT IF IT DOESN'T WORK OUT? ...BUT WHAT IF IT *DOES*?

We talked through the negative mindset and I helped her refocus on the positives. I kept reminding her that she could do this. She had me as a sounding board for all the things that could go wrong—or right. I asked her questions and helped her figure out what barriers and obstacles she'd be facing, with either option. Women can be each other's coaches—and we should—because we all go through times of indecision and fear. Having someone in your corner is essential.

Everyone needs to learn to embrace change. The pandemic's effect on our economy and millions of jobs, as well as the abrupt shift to technology that came about as a result, is a huge lesson in how we need to be okay with learning new skills. The people who aren't afraid to try new things are the ones that will find opportunities, no matter what is going on with the world. They will have the confidence and the ability to reimagine themselves and carve out a new path.

EVERYONE NEEDS TO LEARN TO EMBRACE CHANGE.

A SELF INVESTMENT DEPOSIT SLIP

Cross-training not only prepares you physically to move into a new job, it prepares you mentally. Look at it as building your can-do muscles.

CHAPTER FIVE
THE ROAD LESS TAKEN

A Mulligan.

In golf, it's a do-over. You made a mistake, you ask for a Mulligan, and you try again. For me, that word isn't just my last name, it has also always meant taking a new path when the one I was on stopped leading where I wanted it to go. Getting pregnant in high school derailed the plans I thought I would have after graduation, so I made a new plan. When the company I was working for didn't have a vertical path for my career, I moved horizontally to a new company and created a new path.

Are you at a crossroads in your life? Or wondering why things went left instead of right? Instead of dwelling, the best thing to do is a do-over. It can be scary, yes, but it can also be the best decision you ever made.

I remember being terrified the first time I went door-to-door, selling Girl Scout cookies. It was a huge step out of my comfort zone because I was such a shy kid. I could have seen it as an impossible task or avoided it entirely, instead I chose to do my best.

Life has a way of preparing you for those moments. When I was six or seven, I walked a mile and a half to school. I had really humble beginnings as a child. I moved to different schools around Hillsborough County in Florida, including one in middle school where some of the kids carried guns. I made new friends every time because I figured out how I fit into the new environment and worked to stay caught up with the curriculum at the new school. It was a constant do-over for me, which prepared me to do it again and again as an adult.

People ask me all the time where I get my entrepreneurial spirit from, and I think it's a combination of that background and a family with more than one entrepreneur in it. I have family members who have made their living farming, others who did it through real estate—both of which are mercurial industries that can shift in an instant. That taught me to stay focused and keep swimming.

JUST KEEP MOVING FORWARD. NO MATTER WHAT.

As a solo mom with sole custody, I had to quickly learn to be ready to take a detour when my daughter got sick, or work plans changed, or my boss asked me to take a trip. There were dozens of times that I had to regroup, re-plan, and often ask for help. It taught me to be okay with asking for support as well as how to assess a situation quickly, whether it was with a customer, work, or my child, and then make a plan and follow through.

DON'T WORRY ABOUT WHAT PEOPLE THINK

When I started telling people I was starting Mulligan Financial in the midst of a pandemic, I received a lot of questioning looks and doubts. Not only was I a woman branching out on my own into a male-dominated industry, I was also doing it during a time when the country was rumored to be economically falling apart.

My answer? *Just watch me.*

For so many things that women do, there is no guidebook and no plan. Women are breaking glass ceilings everywhere and pioneering industries and products no one else has before. To do that, they have to ignore the naysayers and keep plowing forward.

It helps to have a really strong *Why* that fuels your journey. For me, it has always been my daughter. From the second she was born, I wanted to give her the life that I never had. I wanted to make sure she had a comfortable life, and a college fund, and vacation experiences. I wanted the best for her, as all parents do, and that became the foundation behind every move I made.

IT HELPS TO HAVE A REALLY STRONG *WHY* THAT FUELS YOUR JOURNEY.

When the real estate market crashed, I moved to Chicago in search of a job. It was 2009 and my daughter was just seven or eight. My parents begged me not to go, but I knew my best opportunity for a job in banking was in a huge city. I had so many OMG moments as I loaded up the U-Haul truck. I'd just gotten divorced, the market was crashing, and I didn't have a job lined up yet. Not to mention, I was moving to a dreary and cold state. But I was determined to make it work, so I took a job I was overqualified for just to get my foot in the door.

Was I scared? Of course I was. I had no family around me, I didn't know anyone, and I had to figure out how to use the transit system, find a nanny, and build a career. We eventually settled in Lincoln Park and my daughter enrolled in a school for the arts. We had a great time there, learning the city and experiencing all the sports and culture. I learned to lean on the people around me for advice and support.

IT'S OKAY TO BE THE ODD DUCK

When it became clear I needed to make another move to climb up the corporate ladder, I took a job in Michigan. All of a sudden, I had to do everything all over again—buy a car, find a nanny, find schools. When I first got there, I didn't have a babysitter and brought my daughter on the interview. She sat in the lobby with the receptionist while I went about securing our new life.

Within thirty days, I had negotiated a relocation deal, we had a brand-new car, and moved into a small town in another very cold state with a big cultural shift. Small town life was an entirely different experience for both of us. This was the kind of town where people married their high school sweethearts and stayed in that town to raise their children. My daughter and I were the odd ones out. People questioned me about why I moved there and why I didn't have a husband. It was an entirely different world from what I knew.

I was lonely there for a long time. Small towns can be very insular and it was surprising to me that I couldn't make friends as easily as I had before. It was yet another step out of my comfort zone, but I grew so much from taking it. By the time I moved back to Florida, I was more resilient and fearless than when I left and more able to take on any challenge.

In the wake of this pandemic, I advise women to be fearless. Do not be afraid to take on something that may be new or an underemployment opportunity.

As long as there is room to move up, keep your eyes focused on what's down the road, not just what's in front of you. Be okay with packing up and moving if you need to.

BE FEARLESS. YOU ARE STRONGER THAN YOU THINK.

Each step you take out of your comfort zone builds strength, just like each rep at the gym. It helps you become prepared for the other storms that come your way, and to know you can survive far more than you know. Staying where you're comfortable doesn't help you grow—it keeps you stagnant.

ENCOURAGE RISK TAKING

When I was helping my sister buy her house, I encouraged her to take that risk. I reminded her that she has wisdom and drive, and that she can do this as a single mom. If you are having doubts about taking the road less traveled, try to see it as a springboard that can launch you into a new level.

That's the approach I took when I was asked to be the coach of the cheerleading team in the Fishhawk community. I didn't know a thing about cheerleading, let alone how to manage a whole squad of teenage angst and emotions. My neighbor Kelly had coached before and told me she would support me.

I spent a lot of time learning routines and practices, actively listening and coaching and giving feedback. It was a good outlet for me as much as it was for the girls. It was a way to stay connected to the community, stay physically fit while working full time, and connect with my daughter. It was also one more thing that I never imagined myself doing—yet I accomplished it all the same. It built my confidence in new ways.

I took a different road from my friends when I left high school, but it didn't stop me from going after my dreams. I knew I had only one direction—forward. That's the same thinking I'm using as I create my own company.

So many men I met were naysayers who told me I couldn't do this on my own. That I needed to move in with them or let them financially support me. They told me I needed a man to help pick out a car and find a great place to live. No, I didn't. I managed to do all of it by myself, and I did it well. I just had to start with believing that I could.

BELIEF IN YOURSELF IS KEY.
KEEP BELIEVING AND MOVING FORWARD.

It was built inside me from the day I was born that I was going to figure it out. At one point when I first got to Chicago and couldn't find a job, I thought I was going to be selling mattress pad protectors. That was okay with me. I was going to do what it took to provide for my daughter and get us off on the right financial foot.

Too often we get caught up in our heads, and our own fears. Don't discount and discredit your strengths. How can those be applied to a new career? A new location? A new industry?

Reach out to other people who are there and ask them for their recipe for success. Chances are good they're going to love giving advice and a nudge in the right direction. Sometimes, all you need is a cheerleader in your corner telling you, '*You can do this. You've got this. You're going to be fine.*'

YOU'VE GOT THIS!

The best cheerleader you have is yourself—so start letting her voice be the loudest.

A SELF INVESTMENT DEPOSIT SLIP

Mantras work great for helping you through scary times or new ventures. Come up with a statement that you can repeat to yourself over and over to restore your confidence. *You've got this, you can do it*…whatever you need to hear, use that as your own internal cheering squad!

CHAPTER SIX
KNOW YOUR WORTH

In the financial world, net worth is an easy thing to calculate by just adding up your assets (bank accounts, real estate, personal property) and then subtracting your liabilities (loans and other debts). Do the math and you arrive at a number that equals your net worth. It's quantifiable.

Personal worth, however, is another thing altogether. Most of us have trouble knowing our self-worth because there is no easy formula for that. However, in order to be strong, empowered women, we have to start by knowing that we are valuable humans with unique skills and characteristics. When you know that—and I mean really know it, deep in your heart—you react to situations from a place of strength, not weakness.

REACT FROM A PLACE OF STRENGTH, NOT WEAKNESS.

A few months ago, someone came to me with a job opportunity. It sounded like a great position, with some interesting aspects, but when the person told me the base salary, I shook my head. I said that I hadn't worked for that kind of salary since I was in my teens and my experience and credentials were worth more than that number. I was able to walk away, knowing I had toed that line in the sand and stood up for myself. Another time, I was going in as a new hire and had to negotiate a relocation package and car allowance as part of my benefits. I asked for those two things, plus stock options, telling the people on the other side of the table, '*Yes, I know what those are and I deserve them*.' I wasn't afraid to ask for more than what they were offering—and I was successful in the end.

When you are downsized, it can be hard to remember what you're worth because being laid off or fired can be a huge hit to your self-esteem. I worked for a Fortune 500 company that went through a massive downsizing and I had to work with each employee on their exit package. It was a tough job because it was difficult to deliver that kind of news. What many women don't realize is that they *can* negotiate their exit package. You can ask for more severance or an extension of benefits. Use those same powers of negotiation to take care of yourself and your family in times of difficulty, too.

In general, women struggle with asking for a salary commensurate with their abilities. We tend to be non-confrontational and hesitant in negotiations. I had an employee who had moved as far up in the company as she could. She knew she deserved a bigger salary but she was afraid to make the leap. I encouraged her to go ahead and make that leap because she had to do what was best for her family, her situation, and herself. Even though she would no longer be in my employ, she had earned and deserved that next step up in her career and a higher salary.

REVALUE WHAT WORTH IS

For centuries, we have attached a dollar sign to worth. I think that's part of what keeps women stuck in the fear of asking for more money.

YOUR WORTH ISN'T JUST WHAT'S ON YOUR RESUME.

Do you have specific industry knowledge? Do you have a strong skillset in your area? Are you great at connecting or negotiating? Those skills and the years of personal experience that go with them, are valuable. Knowing how valuable they are gives you the ammunition to ask for a raise or pursue a more lucrative job.

Before you go into financial negotiations, try doing these things:

1. Use technology to do your research. Google average salaries for your type of position and experience level.

2. Make use of your professional networks. Don't be afraid to ask people who are in similar situations questions like: *Were you able to negotiate a sign-on bonus? What benefits were you offered? Did they add in a relocation package or a car allowance?*

3. Determine whether you are accepting an offer because it's fair or because it's a security blanket. If you deserve more, then push back diligently and delicately with a fair counter offer, mentioning all of those skillsets that might not be on your resume.

REMEMBER, *EVERYTHING* IS NEGOTIABLE.

You shouldn't be the girl who is sent for coffee or to print copies. By standing up for what you are worth before you are even hired, you send the message that you bring *value* to the company. People will see you and your skills in a different light if you give off that vibe of being an important part of the company.

PIVOTING WITH POWER

During the recent pandemic, more and more people have had to shift into different industries or become creative with how they run their companies and do their jobs. People who were behind the scenes workers are now on video calls and the extroverts who loved in-person meetings are working from home. It's been a tough road, and with the high unemployment numbers, many women are finding themselves moving into new careers in order to keep working.

It can be scary to change industries, but if you look at your overall skillsets—*Are you a good networker? Are you a great leader? Do you pay attention to the details?*—those skills often translate well and easily into other careers. A friend of mine left banking and went into commercial real estate. Using her contacts and networks to build her sales base, she was able to become a powerhouse in real estate in a short amount of time.

In a time of change, it's a good idea to dig deep into the skills that you already have. Make a list of your strengths. If you're having trouble naming them, ask your support team for input. Women tend to be so self-critical that we are often blind to all the fabulous skills we have. If you're in an interview or a new job situation, and you don't have the answers, it's completely okay to admit that. I just say, *'That's a great question. Give me some time and I'll get back to you.'*

YOU DON'T HAVE TO BE PERFECT.

If you find yourself in a new industry, try not to feel daunted or overwhelmed. You can and will thrive. During a transitional period between jobs in the banking industry, I went to work for a title company. I had no idea how much there was to learn about that field or how it worked, not to mention the constant pressures to perform and to close. I knew this wouldn't be something I would enjoy long term, so I made the shift back into banking. However, a deeper understanding of the title world gave me another strength when I returned to the financial industry. Take what you learn, even if it's from a stepping-stone job, and leverage that into your next position.

We also need more women to have a voice in all industries. Serving on a board or working within an organization is a great way to help move the needle for all of us. Use your voice to demonstrate the worth that women can bring to the table. That kind of work has a nice ripple effect throughout all industries and communities.

TRAIN THE NEXT GENERATION

Working with the cheer team, I saw firsthand how pressured young girls are to be perfect and fit in. They're constantly peppered with messages from advertising, television, and most of all social media. Those images of "perfection" can quickly erode a girl's self-esteem. Because of that, helping a teenage girl understand her worth is challenging.

Self-doubt came with the territory with the cheer team, whether those insecurities were about weight, looks, or knowing the routine. I worked to be a constant positive reinforcement in their lives by reminding them of the strengths they had, the things they did well, and the long-term goals they had. I learned a lot of those inner-strength and confidence pieces when I was in Girl Scouts and wanted the girls to leave the team with more of both.

You've got this was something I said all the time. Building them up was far more important to me than breaking them down. I reminded them that bad days don't last, and that prom isn't the most important thing in life. That they were working toward bigger things and that they were really just competing against themselves and those inner voices even though it felt like they were competing against other girls.

YOU'VE GOT THIS.

Adult women need to hear that as much as teenage girls do. When you struggle to believe in yourself, it's important to course-correct. It's far too easy to get mired in an endless cycle of negative thinking.

I've gone through many setbacks, both personal and professional. In the midst of a setback, it can be hard to focus on the horizon, but try to keep reminding yourself that all storms pass and setbacks are always temporary.

When something good happens, don't be afraid to celebrate. It's completely okay to take yourself out to lunch or dinner, buy yourself a new pair of shoes, or even buy that private jet if you have the means. Women sometimes feel guilty about self-care and they shouldn't. If your friend worked hard and achieved a difficult goal, you would have celebrated that with her—so treat yourself the same way.

SUPPORT, DON'T UNDERMINE

In the business world, women can be just as catty and hurtful as men. There's not always going to be a club of women that are cheering each other on at work. That's just not real life. Teenage girls need to know what behavior to look out for and how to set boundaries, better they learn that sooner rather than later.

Whatever choices you make in your life—own them and be proud. Historically, women get married, settle down, have a couple of kids, and live in a house in the suburbs. That might be society's expectation, but it doesn't have to be yours. I had to learn how to plow forward as a strong, independent, single woman and to ignore the people who asked me why I wasn't married or who expected me to fit into a particular box.

When you already have your worth built up inside yourself, you'll look at those words differently. You'll see the positives in your life—like I have more

flexibility and autonomy because I'm not married—
and you'll learn to stand up for your choices.

Susan Blackburn is a good friend of mine. She was
the CEO of a community bank in my hometown.
I didn't work with her but, as I got to know her, I
respected and admired her positive outlook on life
and business. She was an encouraging person to be
around, and I believe that kind of attitude rubs off on
others. With the cheerleading team, I learned from the
best cheerleader I knew, Kelly Vasbinder Ratcliff, my
assistant coach. She was patient and supportive and
taught me everything I needed to know to lead those
young women to championships.

Ask yourself if you want to have a positive or negative
impact on the people who are around and coming
up behind you. It's your choice whether to be an
encourager or a detractor. In a world that already has
enough detours and setbacks and judgment, isn't it
better to be a cheerleader than a complainer? Be part
of another woman's support system and help her see
her value in the world.

A SELF INVESTMENT DEPOSIT SLIP

Try these steps the next time your confidence wavers:

1. **Identify** your negative thoughts.

2. **Rewrite** them with positive self-talk. Learn to **recognize** and **replace** those words with can-do words.

3. If you're still struggling, reach out to your **support** network. They're there to cheer you on when you need it most.

CHAPTER SEVEN
SURROUND YOURSELF WITH GOOD COACHES

When you're working with teenage girls, it's easy to get frustrated or snap back at them. They are, after all, teenagers, complete with all the attitude and angst that comes with that age group. However, their self-confidence is shaky at that age, and the worst thing you can do is constantly criticize and be harsh with them.

Encouragement is not scolding; it's not criticizing. Encouragement is giving people the opportunity to learn, then stepping back and watching them grow and flourish. I found the same thing in parenting— the more I was able to use positive reinforcement and encouragement, the more my daughter flourished. If you micromanage anything, it won't have a chance to fully bloom, so learn to take a step back and trust.

IF YOU MICROMANAGE THOSE AROUND YOU, THEY'LL NEVER FULLY BLOOM.

That didn't mean that I didn't have a calendar or structure. Those are vital to achieving your goals and to give you an opportunity to look at the big picture and the far-off goals you are trying to reach. When any of my teams felt discouraged by a loss or a bad day, I tried to help them see the horizon instead of what was right in front of them. We talked about what might need to be eliminated or what might need to be improved in order to reach that point. After the mistake is made, berating a team member doesn't undo the past. The best you can do is help them improve for the future. By having the discussion with them, not yelling at them, you get their investment in the future, too.

TRUST AND VERIFY

Sometimes when you step back and let people try things on their own…the project doesn't go quite as expected, especially in a team environment. I had a client who needed a banker to help her with a big transaction. I brought together a banker I knew, my client, the lender, and the client's CFO on a call. These people are all representations of me, so there was a lot of trust involved in this connection.

After the call, I followed up with an email to my client and outlined the next steps. My client replied and said the bank hadn't sent the promised Dropbox file to take those next steps. It could have been a disaster, a moment where my client felt let down by the banker, but I had paid attention during the call and taken notes. I reminded my client that the banker said her CFO had to add the banker to the Dropbox folder in order to share the documents. I trusted the team I had put together, but I also had oversight and direction when it was needed, preventing a chaotic outcome.

In negotiations and business, I am always straightforward, direct, with no fluff. I find that approach works well in business, especially when you are working with dominating personalities, whether they are male or female. I don't yell or criticize, but I am strong and sure in my responses and unafraid to stand up for what is right.

STAND STRONG WHEN YOU NEED TO; ENCOURAGE WHEN OTHERS NEED YOU TO.

That straightforward, strong approach has worked well to establish me as a leader. When I decided to go out on my own and start Mulligan Financial, I was surprised at how many people I had known over the course of my career who said they believe in me, embraced what I was doing, and told me I could do whatever I put my mind to doing, whether it be banking or politics (trust me, I'm not getting into politics!). That gave me the boost I needed when I was making a huge change.

HOW TO FIND THE RIGHT MENTOR

Mentors are everywhere, if you look hard enough. For instance, LinkedIn has this great group called the Leadership Group, which had an offshoot called the Leadership Mentor Group. There are mentor groups on Instagram, Snapchat, Facebook. You can find some on professional networking sites. Or reach out to someone who has connected mentors and mentees in the past. I have people who have reached out to me and asked about the best way to find someone who can encourage and guide them.

> *A mentorship is a give and take*: Like any relationship, this is not a one-way street. You don't just take all that advice and not give in return. Thank your mentor and ask in return how you can help him or her? Remember, this person is giving you their time and energy, and even if they charge a fee (some do), you should be looking for ways to give back. That's the world of commerce, and knowledge is a form of currency. It can be as simple as an *I appreciate you* note or call, a lunch with nothing but good conversation, or as big as

promoting their next event. Make sure you have no agenda in your thank-you actions.

Give to the people behind you: We all got where we are because someone opened a door or gave us a bit of knowledge. If you want a better world, then be a part of making it better by helping those who are coming up behind you in your industry. We're all here for the greater good, so let's show that through supporting each other.

Look at who surrounds you: Your support system is vital, so look closely at who you have in your circle. Are they supportive people? Do they reinforce your self-doubt or encourage you? Have they been successful in their own right? Do they create a can-do environment with the people they interact with?

At my core, I love to help people solve problems. My drive and motivation come from that basic part of my personality, which is why I'm so passionate about helping people achieve their financial goals and reach that next level.

BE A MENTOR PERSONALITY

Because of that desire to help people, I look for opportunities to show support. For instance, there's a small restaurant that has done business with me before. I knew they weren't doing well during the pandemic closures, so whenever I had to schedule a meeting in that area, I held it at that restaurant as a way to help support them.

In the beginning of my career, I hesitated to reach out to other business owners for advice. I didn't value what I brought to the table and it took time for me to learn that I had skills and strengths that others could benefit from as well. It took trust, not just in the people I work with, but in myself. Now, I try to do that with other people. When they doubt their ability to achieve a goal, I try to do a lot of confidence rebuilding and re-instilling in the way I talk to that person.

Be that dependable person whom others can look to when they need a helping hand. Reach out to them once in a while or find opportunities to support their business. Give to those relationships as much as you can because that creates success for everyone. A team success is so much sweeter than an individual achievement!

> YOU'RE ONLY AS GOOD AS YOUR FOLLOW-UP
> AND YOUR RELATIONSHIPS WITH OTHER PEOPLE.

BECOME SOMEONE OTHERS ADMIRE

There were so many people along the way who were my role models as I was working my way up in the industry. I saw these women who did it all and did it well, and thought, *'If they can do it, so can I.'*

You never know when someone else is watching your actions. Be a role model in all ways, at all times, because chances are good there is another woman who wants to be you when she grows up. You can live by example and influence people simply by being yourself.

When I mentor others, I talk to them about their strengths and weaknesses, and help them pinpoint those things within themselves. Several times, there have been people who came to me when they were at a crossroads, trying to decide which way to go with their career. Being on the outside, I was able to give them that pros and cons list that helped them make the decision that was best for them and their family.

I often use my own history to help encourage other women. I want them to know that they can do hard things, that they can balance their family and their career, and that they can take big risks that pay off. The teenage girls on the cheer team had to learn to trust in their training, their coach, and their teammates. As adults, women need to learn to do the same.

One more tip—mentoring doesn't have to be a boring meeting. Go play a round of golf or a game of tennis with your mentor or mentee. Engage and interact and laugh. Having fun can loosen people up a little bit and get them to be more forthright as well as more open to new ideas. Life is serious enough—let the next adventure of your life start with fun!

A SELF INVESTMENT DEPOSIT SLIP

Mentorship is a lot like parenting: How are you, where are you going, who are you surrounding yourself with, what's your timeline to complete this goal?

If you don't have a mentor right now, then ask yourself these questions on a regular basis. Do a weekly check-in to see if you're heading down the path toward your next great thing!

CHAPTER EIGHT

DON'T SWEAT
THE COMPETITION

The day before our first major competition, the girls on the cheer squad were nervous. They had seen the other teams compete and knew they were up against some tough squads. In practice the day before, the basket catches failed twice and that left the girls feeling insecure, uncertain, and worried about their performance.

I could see the doubt on their faces, so I gathered them into a circle and had each girl give the one next to her a compliment on her skills. As they went around the circle, I heard, "*You're a great flyer. You're a strong base. You always encourage others.*" I could see their confidence begin to return. They were supporting each other and building each other up, which built a stronger team.

LEAN INTO YOUR STRENGTHS

I reminded the girls that not every girl was made equally, and that was a good thing because it meant they could move into positions that were their strengths. A girl might want to be a flyer but her strengths were in being part of the base, and her contribution to the team was just as important as anyone else's.

For some girls, knowing their areas of strength was difficult. Teenage girls are notoriously insecure and tend to engage in a lot of self-criticism, masking the positive skillsets they possess. I had to watch them and pay attention to where they excelled, and then coach each girl slightly differently to tease out those strengths and help her find her confidence.

That comes into play in the workplace, too. I often get asked about the teams I have built and how I assembled a group of people who worked well together. For me, it's about building great relationships with the people I work with. That gives me the chance to get to know them, see whether they are a better networker or organizer, and how they mesh with other people. It's exactly the same process I used with the cheer squad, only the stage is a workplace instead of a mat.

UNDERSTAND WHAT YOUR STRENGTHS ARE AND LEAN INTO THEM. LEARN
TO UTILIZE YOUR STRENGTHS, BOTH ON YOUR OWN AND ON A TEAM.

Too often, people don't spend enough time observing. They jump into action and that rush to move forward can result in mistakes. Observation and analysis help you make decisions that are measured, which ultimately results in a better success rate.

BREAK BAD HABITS

Sometimes it's easier to build a team from scratch, but I've often been brought in to work with an existing team. That observation period is vital because it helps you see the positives and negatives of the group. I let them show off their skills and give them an opportunity to tell me what they think they are best at. Sometimes, they're spot-on, and sometimes they're not. I've often run into people who are set in their ways and don't even want to consider a change.

BE OPEN TO NEW OPPORTUNITIES AND POSITIONS.

If you want to be successful at anything, you have to be willing to learn and take risks. If a manager or owner is telling you that you have skills at speaking, for instance, don't let nerves or the fact that you've always worked behind the scenes keep you from stepping out of your comfort zone.

You'll also gain valuable cross-training—we have talked about this before—which makes you more marketable and able to switch gears when necessary. See whatever strengths you have as a positive feature about yourself and build on them. Then, turn and do the same for the woman beside you, just as I did with the team—tell another woman what you see as her strengths. By building each other up instead of always competing, we can create a positive environment that encourages growth.

It also helps you in times of doubt. I remember the girls watching videos of other teams competing and it made them feel inadequate. I started videotaping my team's practices, then showing them how they had grown and changed from week to week. It helped them see how far they had come—and how far they could grow— which built their confidence. If you are struggling to see your strength in speaking or negotiating, have someone record you so you can see if maybe you are perceiving failure when you're actually doing great!

AVOID THE RUTHLESS ONES

In any setting, other women can be ruthless, undercutting and undermining the "competition" at work. I've seen it and experienced that many times. The key is to know who you are, stick to that core being, and when in doubt, go to the people who know and support you because they will help you see the real you that's shining through.

> ## WE NEED TO BE STRONGER IN UNITY, RATHER THAN WEAKER IN THE DIVIDE.

During the recent pandemic, it would have been really easy for the women I know to just stay in their own lanes, especially since so many of us were working from home and cut off from each other. Instead, these strong women I am friends with kept reaching out and supporting each other. They were there for each other, regardless of what was going on.

Men can also be competitive with each other and with women. That ruthlessness isn't limited to one gender. The same advice applies—know your strengths and your value and don't let the ruthless sharks make you falter.

YOU'RE ONLY COMPETING WITH YOURSELF

I recently played putt-putt golf with my parents and noticed my mother is not only good at the game, she's a bit competitive, too, just like me. She doesn't, however, try to compete with me or my father—she competes with herself. She wants to be better at this hole than the one before, or end up with a lower score than she had the last time we played.

Competing with yourself can be healthy, if you are doing an honest self-evaluation and striving to be better than the day before. Ask yourself:

- Are you happy with where you are in terms of your goals and performance?

- Are there areas you'd like to improve?

- Are you getting distracted by focusing on your competition instead of yourself?

- What's one thing you can do today to be better than yesterday?

The foundational skills I talked about earlier—practice, discipline, and focus—are the keys to becoming better every day at whatever you are doing. If your focus is on other people and what they are doing, you'll no doubt be distracted. It's like driving down the highway and only paying attention to the car in the next lane. If you do that too long, you'll crash or run off the road.

FOCUS ON YOUR LANE AND YOUR ULTIMATE DESTINATION.

Today's culture sets us up for failure because we are constantly bombarded with images and social media messages that say we are somehow lacking because we don't drive this or wear that. That's all about advertising, not about anything that is lacking in you or better with another person. So much of competition is really our own minds sending us negative messages. In all honesty, other people aren't thinking about you and me—they're worrying about themselves.

My industry is highly competitive. Every bank is doing the same thing—competing for the money that people and businesses have to invest. The industry inspires competition and I've seen people break under that constant internal pressure to perform well.

Learning to decompress and refocus is vital. Sometimes, at the end of the day, I come home, sit down, and just kind of reflect on the day. It's like a natural meditation for me. I don't need a beach or a yoga mat, I just need to take a breath and give my day a non-judgmental analysis. Then I can decide what areas need to be tweaked or what things I can do to move the goal forward.

When I first took on the cheer team, I reached out to other coaches. Yes, we were competing against these teams but, at the end of the day, they're another cheer team facing a lot of the same challenges we were. We commiserated and shared some strategies and supported each other. When I went to a competition, there were friendly faces across the room and all because I decided to put those few hours of competition aside and become a source of support instead.

That's what women need to do more of—build teams and networks instead of trying so hard to beat the person next to you. Refocus on yourself and on where you are going, then fill your life with the people who are the best teammates to help you get there!

A SELF INVESTMENT DEPOSIT SLIP

Who are you? Are you the leader, the negotiator, or the communicator? Sit back and identify who you are and what role you serve. Don't judge yourself because of what skills you lack—celebrate yourself for all those awesome strengths you have.

Or, think of yourself as a team. When you have a team of people, you know and work within their individual strengths. What team of strengths do you bring to the table?

- Teacher
- Leader
- Motivator
- Guide
- Facilitator
- Software guru
- Trailblazer

If you're weak in one area, partner with people who complement your strengths. Together, you can do even more!

CHAPTER NINE

DEALING WITH SETBACKS

I watched the cheerleader in front of me thrust her arms in front of her and then jump up, trying to bring her legs to meet her outstretched hands. Over and over again, she tried to do the pike, and over and over again, she failed. She was frustrated and on the verge of tears when I went over to talk to her.

It can be daunting when you fail over and over again. This girl, like so many of us, started to think there was something wrong with her because she just couldn't get it right. I told her exactly what I'm going to tell you right now:

THERE IS NOTHING WRONG WITH YOU. SETBACKS HAPPEN.

Pick yourself up and try again. Most of all, accept that some days everything will work out perfectly and nothing will seem to go right on other days. But just like storms pass, bad days and setbacks do, too.

IT'S NOT JUST YOU

During the pandemic, so many people struggled to keep their heads above water. The worldwide economic shutdown impacted every single industry. Deep down, we all know that others are suffering too, but when you're struggling to cover the rent check or have applied for dozens of jobs and haven't found one yet, it feels like a personal failure.

Start by knowing that you are not alone—and that other people have overcome and triumphed. Because of that, you can too.

Next, be open to doing things in a new way. The Covid-19 pandemic forced many companies to pivot and become more virtual or start whole new revenue streams. Some, sadly, had to close entirely. Others consolidated debts, refinanced, and redirected their energies. They got creative and found a way to thrive amid the chaos. How?

THEY SAW THEIR SETBACK AS AN OPPORTUNITY, NOT A FAILURE.

The people who can adapt and reinvent themselves will be the ones who thrive. They are open to new ideas and stay attuned to what is going on in their industry and the world. They adapt to change and they prevail.

ADAPT AND BREATHE

For some people, switching to a work at home environment has been a big struggle. Learning the new technology, staying self-motivated, juggling dogs and kids and laundry—all of these things can make a change like that difficult. We are all going through a disruption and change of some sort right now, whether it's learning to buy groceries through an app or homeschooling, people are having to reinvent how they do everything in their lives.

The people who accept these changes are the ones who ride the rough waters easily. I'm not saying that's going to be easy—but it is possible. No matter your age, industry, or experience level, you can adapt and change.

TAKE A DEEP BREATH AND KNOW IT WILL BE OKAY.

I look around me and see women supporting other women in technology or referring them to helpful websites. I'm using those resources to educate myself, too. There are major changes in every decade and the changes become second nature as we learn to accept them and shift our thinking and ways of doing business,. For example, think about something as simple as the cash payment apps on our phones. Who would have thought we would send money to each other through an app like Venmo, Zelle, or Cash? The invention of those types of applications revolutionized banking. These changes in the world will revolutionize other industries, and maybe us, too.

SURROUND YOURSELF WITH POSITIVITY

When you are going through turmoil, the last thing you want to do is wallow in the mud. It's totally fine to take a moment to mourn what was or to express trepidation about the next steps, but the sooner you can pick yourself up and move on, the better off you'll be. A big part of doing that is your support network. Take a look at the people around you. Are they:

- Positive: If your friends see the glass as half-empty, they're not going to be that pick-me-up voice you need during a setback. Look for the optimists in your group.

- Driven: Friends who are driven encourage others to be driven as well. They also often have that can-do attitude in the midst of chaos. Lean on these people for advice and encouragement.

- Honest: As much as the truth can be difficult to hear, it's also often necessary. Do you have friends who will speak freely with you? The ones who will say, *Hey, you've been moping about this long enough, let's do something about it now.*

- Supportive: These are the people who remind you that you are capable and accomplished in the moments when you feel you aren't. The girls on the cheer team would whoop and clap for the girls who tried hard, even if they didn't stick the landing or complete the stunt. A good team of friends supports and cheers you on.

At the same time as you are making use of your support group, institute a set of checks and balances with yourself. What is the reality of where you are professionally? Where do you stand financially? Resume wise? Personally? What do you need to make or need to do in order to survive? By looking at your situation with realistic and objective lenses, it's easier to make the choices you have to make, whether it's relocating or retraining.

I've had times in my career when I've had to start all over. Other times when I had to put up boundaries so that I could focus on my career and not on what other people needed. I stayed where I was to finish what I had to do before I went to that event or had that meeting.

Leaders do this well. They analyze the truth of the situation, then set their priorities and put up whatever boundaries are necessary in order to keep the ship moving forward. They also look for the positive in the negative—what good things are coming out of this setback or detour? What lessons am I learning?

How will this help me or the company grow? Competition is fierce, whether you are in sales or cheerleading. Those failures can be so disheartening, but if you take a moment to think about what went well, what didn't, and what you can change going forward, you'll do far better than if you dwell on the defeat.

Look at the leaders in your industry and analyze what they are doing right. Are they networking a lot on LinkedIn? Making more calls? Having better interaction with the clients? What impression are they leaving behind? Are they connecting? Showing compassion? Do they have a good understanding of the clients' needs and being consultative instead of just trying to sell?

These are lessons you can learn from and that can help you adapt and change with the next step in your journey. Don't discourage yourself. Encourage yourself, just as you would with someone you are mentoring.

GIVE YOURSELF PERMISSION TO WORRY

Change is hard. Change is scary. While you don't want to stay caught in a pattern of fear and anxiety, it is totally okay to have a moment of *what do I do now*? Learn to lean into that feeling of being overwhelmed or nervous. And when it's needed, take a day off to recharge. Go sit by the pool, listen to your favorite music, and give your brain a vacation from the worry. Sometimes, the best ideas come when we are simply being without overthinking and overanalyzing.

Opening your mind also removes the fences around your plans. You are capable of doing more than one thing in this world, of having more than one career. Go back to your core strengths—connector, organizer, coach, leader, risktaker—and see what other opportunities fit your personality type.

BE WILLING TO MOVE IN A NEW DIRECTION.

Being open to new opportunities, even if they are out of your comfort zone, means letting go of those staunch "must" and "should" statements. It's about saying, *I can do this* and giving yourself the grace to fail a few times before you get it right.

ATTITUDE IS EVERYTHING

I remember a competition where one of my girls stumbled during the routine and took a little fall. Instead of slinking off in embarrassment, she popped back up with a smile and a thumbs-up as if she'd meant to do that. She had a great attitude about her tumble and didn't stress about that one mistake.

Your attitude makes a huge difference in how you respond to stresses and changes. People tell me that I'm a super positive person. I don't know where I get that attitude from, but I think it's an extension of my network. I don't surround myself with negative people, just as you don't fill a rose garden with weeds and expect the roses to grow.

IF YOU WANT TO BRIGHTEN YOUR OUTLOOK, START BY GETTING OUT OF THE SHADOWS.

Having a good attitude *is a choice*. No one makes that choice every day—it's impractical to think that every single day will be sunny-side up. When I was seventeen and pregnant, I had plenty of days when I thought life wasn't fair, that my future was going to be bleak, and that I couldn't do this on my own. I once asked my mom how I got through those difficult years with a newborn baby, and she told me, "You had days that you cried, but you just kept moving forward."

I had to learn how to buckle my chin strap, get out of bed, and make each day great. I learned to look at it as a path that God had me on, for whatever reason, and that He had a bigger plan at play than I couldn't see.

If your attitude is wavering try, to remind yourself of the hard things you have done. You have overcome big obstacles, no matter how old you are. Stop overthinking everything and don't compare yourself to others. Have a little faith that it will all work out as long as you are true to yourself and others.

YOU DON'T HAVE TO HAVE GPS

Remember the days before we had GPS systems in our cars and on our phones? When we got lost, we had to figure out where we were and how to get home. We'd pull out a map, or retrace our steps, or ask for directions. That's what you have to do when you suffer a setback.

YOU ALREADY HAVE ALL THE BUILT-IN SURVIVAL SKILLS YOU NEED.

Whether you are getting lost in the middle of Nebraska or losing your job and finding a new career, you already have the skills you need to solve the problem. It's just like when the network goes down when you need driving directions. What do you do? You think in new directions and are ready to ask for help when necessary. Do that for yourself, too.

A couple years ago, I took a solo road trip up the East coast. I had a few moments of self-doubt—*what if I break down, what if I get lost, what if something happens*—but I kept going. Then I stopped in Hershey, Pennsylvania and did a tour of the chocolate factory there. The docent told us how many times Milton Hershey failed and lost everything before he finally succeeded and became a worldwide phenomenon.

What I took from that was a little of his can-do spirit. I stopped thinking about worst case scenarios. I took the detours along the road and didn't get upset by the setbacks or the adventures. I reconnected with family members and had a fantastic time. The trip taught me that I can move when I need to, rearrange whatever needs to be changed, and most of all, to always be resilient.

DON'T BE AFRAID OF THE RESET.

I've met dozens of women over the years who have lost everything after a job change, a loss of a loved one, or a divorce. They had a reset and they had a choice—to either stay where they were or restart the engine and move in a new direction. Guess which option they chose?

When you have a setback, focus on your values and what is most important to you. Is it faith, family, money, or community? Those are the things that are at the heart and soul of everything we do. They are also the basis of your reset. It's easy to let a setback deteriorate your values. The setback often leaves you emotionally vulnerable and, in those moments, you might waver on what's most important.

I've tried to always stick to my core values of doing good, being good, and building community relationships. To me, values are like eating your fruit every day. A healthy diet is what's required to run a healthy body. Healthy values are what's required to run a healthy company.

I walked into a company the other day and was amazed at the positive culture they had created there. It was clear that the owner had prioritized happy employees in his approach to business. He filled that company with people who brought a variety of pieces together and who knew how to work with each other to get to the next step.

HAVE A FALLBACK PLAN

There have been times when I have had to develop an immediate fallback plan because someone on the cheer team was injured or sick. We always had a backup routine we could do if something happened to the main people on the squad.

You need a fallback plan for your career, too. Don't be afraid to step to the right or take a few steps back if it leads you where you want to go. The path to the top is rarely straight, and sometimes, as I found on my road trip, the detours are the most exciting part of the journey!

A SELF IMPROVEMENT DEPOSIT SLIP

Close your eyes. I want you to visualize the future you want to have. Imagine it happening in every detail, from the office you'll have to the car you'll drive to the people who surround you. See it, believe in it, and know you have everything you need to make it happen. Then write yourself a daily reminder—*You Can Do It!*—and tape it on your mirror or make it your phone's home screen.

CHAPTER TEN
BE READY FOR
THE DISMOUNT

One of the hardest things in cheerleading is the dismount. If you're off on your calculations by a fraction of an inch, the landing can be anything from shaky to disastrous. I taught my girls to plan ahead, to know where they wanted to land and how, so that they could get their body in the right position before they made that final leap. Life works pretty much the same way.

My daughter is grown now and living her own life, which has meant I've had to redefine myself and what I want for my future since I'm no longer a full-time single mom. I've always liked children so, no matter what my life holds going forward, I know I'll be involved in working with young people somehow, whether it's mentoring or coaching. That's part of the planning that is going into my "dismount".

When you're young, thinking about life after kids, after work, after marriage, after whatever path you have pursued, seems impossible. It seems so far in the distance, the days when you are winding down will be here but before you know it and you'll be looking at a landing of your own.

Just as I cautioned my cheerleaders to find other passions to pursue, because the day would come when they wouldn't be able to do a cartwheel, I caution the people I mentor to be multi-directional because different stages of life will require different skillsets and moves. They'll need to be open to new ideas and maybe entirely new starts.

YOU DON'T HAVE TO FIT A STEREOTYPE

Society expects us all to be married, living in the suburbs, and raising two kids. That's not how life works out for everyone, and that is *totally okay*. Not getting married, not living in the suburbs, not having kids—those are all choices that are completely perfect. It doesn't mean there's anything wrong with you because you went in a different direction—it means you are living *your* best life. Not someone else's.

LIVE YOUR OWN BEST LIFE—NOT THE EXPECTATIONS SET BY SOMEONE ELSE.

We also don't have to do the same things our parents or grandparents did. In fact, we can take as many lessons from the older generation as they can from us. They are more technologically and internet savvy, and they often look at the world through a different lens than we do. Be open to new thinking, new ways of doing things, and completely new adventures.

That frees you to try different directions and to not be stuck in the same patterns for decades. I know that change is scary and that some people stick to the predictability of their current situation because it feels safe, but I promise you, taking a leap into an entirely new area will make you stronger and better.

HAVE A DESTINATION IN MIND

When you go on a road trip, you always have an ultimate destination, even if it's where you're going to turn around before you head back home. There has to be a plan in place, otherwise, you'll run out of gas and cash along the way. Nobody wants to end up hitchhiking on a dark road, so they make a plan, even if it's a loose one that allows for detours along the way.

The same should be in place for your own future. Where do you want to end up in ten years? Twenty? Thirty?

Too often, we focus on the immediate moment and not the long-term future, especially when you are young and the future seems like this vague site in the distance. However, if you wait too long to plan ahead, you'll miss the turns you need to take to get to your destination.

I believe there are three kinds of people in the world:

- The person who lays the bricks: this is someone who creates a foundation for their future. They find a secure job, get a savings account, start a retirement fund. They have the bricks in place to hold up the building for a long time.

- The person who earns a living: This is someone who goes to work every day, punches a time clock, and mostly lives paycheck to paycheck. They have some savings, but are focused only on this month's bills, not the ones post-retirement.

- The person who is building a legacy: This is someone who strategizes from the beginning, with smart investments and savings. They look at long-range earning potential, whether that is from stocks, real estate, or other investments. They focus on building wealth that lasts after their death, so that the next generation can have a firm financial foundation.

Which of the three are you? If you're not in the legacy category, then start thinking about how you can shift your focus in order to build generational wealth, rather than just today's savings. Having a plan for the future is really just looking at where you want to be going and seeing how that will all come together.

KNOW YOUR TOOLS

Whenever I talked to the cheerleaders about their post-cheer futures, I focused on the skills that made them great people, not just great cheerleaders. The girl who lifted everyone's spirits after a loss, or the one who made sure everyone arrived on time to a practice, or the one who organized a surprise birthday party for a teammate, all had different skills that will serve them on and off the mat.

What tools and skills do you have in your purse or briefcase? You have everything you need in there already. I think of Michele Pfeifer in *One Fine Day* as one of those people who are prepared for any contingency. She portrays a busy single mom who has a purse the size of Rhode Island. In it, she carries extra shirts and toy cars and crayons. Every single time there is a crisis in that movie, she realizes she has what she needs in her bag. You do too.

EVERYTHING YOU NEED TO HAVE THAT
FUTURE IS ALREADY IN YOUR HANDS.

This is not about titles or bank accounts. It's about knowing who you are as a human being and using those qualities to make your dreams happen. Create your own vision, your own brand, and your own horizon. You don't have to follow any kind of prescribed steps that society puts on you.

HAVE A VISION

One of the great tools for planning ahead is a vision board. It can be written out or full of pictures that you clipped and pasted on the board. However your vision board looks, use it as a way to refocus your attention on the road ahead.

Then start cleaning out the things that weigh you down. As I get older, I find I'm selling more of the things that clutter my life. I'm buying less and investing in experiences and myself. I'm streamlining, so that my path ahead is smoother. Look around you— what things in your life are cluttering your physical, financial, or mental space? Clean them out and make space for your dreams!

I recently sold my golf cart because I realized golf wasn't making me happy. It's something I did because it's what everyone else does. Instead, I took up playing volleyball and I'm loving the change of pace, the freedom, and the fun. I'm ready for my dismount and I'm putting everything I love to do and be on the mat.

When I sat down and envisioned my future, I knew I wanted it to be clean, uncluttered, and filled with experiences. By creating that vision board, I could start to feel and touch that image. Now, when I have to make a purchase or investment decision, I come back to that vision board and ask myself: *Does this fit what I want for my future?*

Don't be afraid of the changes that are to come. Downsizing can be liberating. Starting a new career can be exciting. Moving can be reinvigorating. If you look at it through a positive lens, the entire experience becomes richer and better.

LOOK AROUND YOU

Part of your vision should also encompass the people who fit that ideal future. If you have people in your life who are toxic or negative, clean them out too. They don't fit what you want down the road.

ELIMINATE THE THINGS—AND PEOPLE—THAT WEIGH YOU DOWN.

Finally, add some positive inspiration to your vision board. There are going to be days that seem dark, roads that seem impossible, and you need to remember that you can do this, that you are strong, and that you can weather any storm that hits you.

No matter which direction you go or which way the wind blows you, always be your own best cheerleader. You are worth every minute and dime that you invest in yourself. Know that worth, deep in your bones, and celebrate it, every single day. Go you!

BE YOUR OWN BEST CHEERLEADER. ALWAYS.

A SELF INVESTMENT DEPOSIT SLIP

Are you weighed down by clutter? Does it seem overwhelming to change that situation? Start by just removing one thing per day—one extra dish, one extra dress, one extra book—until the decluttering becomes easier and you can finally start breathing easier in a space that has plenty of room for a fabulous future!

Do You Want to Make an Impact?

NOW Publishing will help you build your book and deliver your message in a powerful, impactful way.

Everyone has a story to tell and NOW Publishing is here to help them bring those stories to life. Whether you have already written a book and need a marketing partner to promote your story, or have an idea for a book that can change lives and inspire others, we are here to help you turn that into something memorable and marketable.

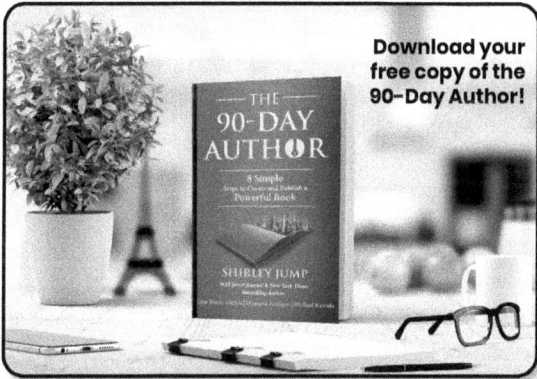

Download your free copy of the 90-Day Author!

THE
90-DAY AUTHOR

8 Simple
Steps to Create and Publish a
Powerful Book

SHIRLEY JUMP

ABOUT THE AUTHOR

Jennifer Mulligan has been interested in the world of commerce ever since she watched her entrepreneurial mother run a successful small business. After becoming a young mother in 2000, Jennifer became adept at structured days, sleepless nights, and continued dedication to her child and her career. She has always worked in the male-dominated industry of banking and rose to the top by being a skilled leader and caring mentor. She specializes in building teams and creating tomorrow's leaders in the financial industry. Jennifer has sat on numerous boards, won multiple awards for leadership, and continues to give back by volunteering for many non-profits. A Tampa native, Jennifer has recently opened her own brokerage firm, helping businesses with debt reduction and financing.

Social Media @YoureTheBestInvestment
Email: mulliganfinancial123@gmail.com
Website: MulliganFinancialService.com